Oneira:
I Dream the Self

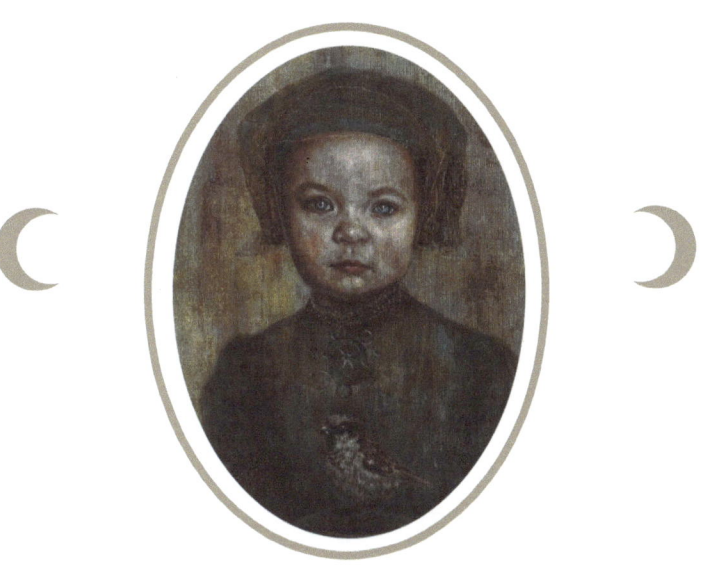

2nd Annual All Women Artists Group Exhibition 2014
May 17 - June 13, 2014

Santa Fe Art Colony 2349 So. Santa Fe Ave. Studio C Los Angeles, CA 90058

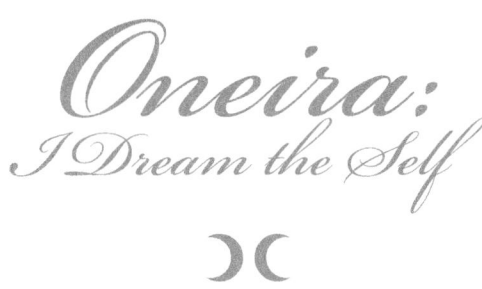

Oneira:
I Dream the Self

)(

2nd Annual All Women Artists Group Exhibition 2014
May 17 - June 13, 2014

Opening Reception: Saturday May 17th, 6 - 9 p.m.
Panel Discussion Sunday May 18th, 1 - 3 p.m.
Moderated by Molly Barnes

Participating Artists:
Kaleeka Bond, Tamara Ann Burgh, Ada Pullini Brown, Shaktima Brien,
Salem Cade, Rowena Hannan, Pamela Hassell, Robin Hextrum, Laura K. Johnston,
Kathryn Jacobi, Eleni Lyra, Mary Ancilla Martinez, Hanneke Naterop, Peggy Nichols,
Robyn Nichols, Star Padilla, Sierra Pecheur, Carolin Peters, Serena Potter,
Linda Rand, Karrie Ross, Lorraine Serena, Betty Shelton, Jill Sykes,
Hope Thier, Page Turner, Shelli Tollman, Melora Walters & Kimberly Webber

Exhibition Juried by & Essays by:
Ada Pullini Brown, Betty Ann Brown & Peggy Nichols

Santa Fe Art Colony 2349 So. Santa Fe Ave. Studio C Los Angeles, CA 90058

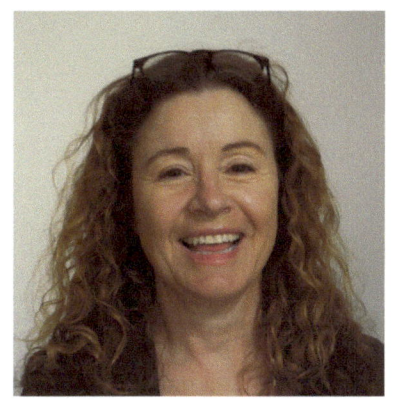

"Come from heaven, wrapped in a purple cloak...Of all
the stars, the loveliest...I spoke to you, Aphrodite,
in a dream."

~Sappho

Dreaming has had a profound influence on my creative life. I can remember dreams as far back as the age of 3. Some of the dreams were euphoric and some were incredibly terrifying. Some were recurring and one, in particular, I had to will out of existence. Yet, I have always been fascinated by dreams. I have recorded them for many years, in journals, sketchbooks, paintings and drawings. This work has been personal and rarely shown.

As I have matured, I have become interested in bringing these works into the light.

It occurred to me, that when I speak about my dreaming, it is more often with other women. As such, I thought it would be interesting to find other women artists that have a similar inclination to draw inspiration from their dreams. To my delight, I have found an incredible group of women artists, whose work embodies beautifully, the mystifying realm of dreaming.

Oneira: I Dream the Self is a group exhibition featuring personal interpretation of dreaming, from a female perspective. The creation from these influences could be by a particular vivid or recurring dream. It could also be a conscious dream, as in something imagined. The dream world of the unconscious mind is the most mysterious, fascinating part of our lives. One-third of our lives is spent sleeping. Nightly we dream, whether we are aware of it or not.

Women have a particular connection to the dream landscape in that women possess a natural infinity to clairvoyance, awareness, healing and intuition.

Artists have been the purveyor of dreams throughout time. It is the intent of the **Oneira** exhibition to explore the realm of dream, imagination and thought, through the unique vision of women artists.

Peggy Nichols
April 2014

Oneira: Dreams and Dreamers

Our truest life is when we are in dreams awake.

~Henry David Thoreau

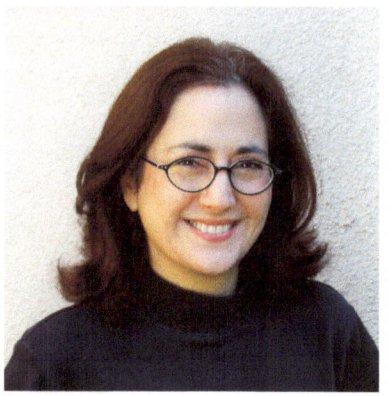

An exhibition space filled with exceptional work of contemporary art is the realized dream of Peggy Nichols. She has nurtured Gallery C to this second annual exhibition with great passion for art and in doing so has realized her goal of featuring the work of women artists. On this success of a "dream awake," we congratulate her and wish her well.

Dreams (in the original Greek: oneiro) are the subject here.

The exhibition gives us a body of work depicting the act of dreaming - the sleeping figure, the coming of consciousness in the trance-like moment of waking from a dream or the phantasmagorical dream itself, each depicted from the unique viewpoint of the artist.

These varied interpretations give the viewer an opportunity to ponder the very thing we all do throughout our lives — we dream. As Shakespeare reminds us in The Tempest, "We are such stuff as dreams are made on, and our little life is rounded with a sleep." Enjoy the exhibition!

Ada Pullini Brown
Associate Professor of Art
Rio Hondo College, Whittier, CA
April 2014

Dream Food: The Artists of Oneira

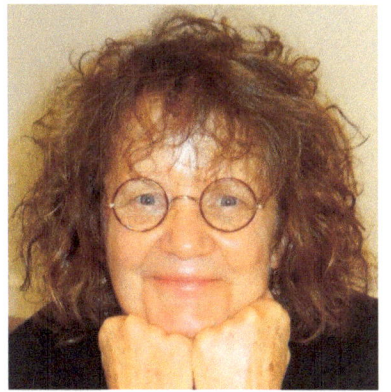

> Our life is composed greatly from dreams, from the unconscious, and they must be brought into connection with action. They must be woven together.
> ~Anais Nin

The artists of **Oneira** weave together their dream images, bringing them into connection with all of us. Several of the artists portray dreamers. In Betty Shelton's evocative painting, a beautiful woman sleeps, wrapped in silvery sheets, and haunted by a ghostly dressmaker's model. In Laura K. Johnston's, a prone figure is sheathed in a gossamer cocoon, with a cluster of sea urchin spikes on its forehead and a carmine tree sprouting from its ear.

Other artists construct images of dreams in complex narrative tableaux. As if in a page out of her dream journal, Peggy Nichols shows us two girls, clad in thin white gowns, as they tumble out of the sky towards a field of crystals. Kathryn Jacobi's canvases are stages for the theater of the absurd, the decapitated, the malformed. Eerie performers strut against a fiery sky that is ripped open by soaring black wings and clouds of pendant breasts.

Still other artists present resonant single images, like "stills" from dreamed "films." In Eleni Lyra's painting, a sleeping woman cuddles into chair, with a tall man hovering behind her. They are veiled behind a billowing curtain. Pamela Hassell's photograph opens into a deep clearing, with a luminescent moon pushing its whitening light up through the flickering branches of a dark forest.

The **Oneira** dreams appear in three dimensions as well. Sierra Pecheur offers raw, labial hearts, their chambers ripped open to reveal dark, shadowed interiors--or golden ones, glossed like jewels. And Robyn Nichols serves up Celtic-interlace silverware beside a plate composed of six sharp leaves ringed by serpentine tendrils. Her table setting exists somewhere between the French Surrealists and Hollywood's Medieval fantasy in Game of Thrones.

Paulo Coelho reminds us that "[w]e must never stop dreaming. Dreams provide nourishment for the soul, just as a meal does for the body." The **Oneira** artists create works that give us precisely that nourishment. Bon appetit!

Betty Ann Brown, Ph.D.
Professor of Art History
California State University, Northridge, CA
April 2014

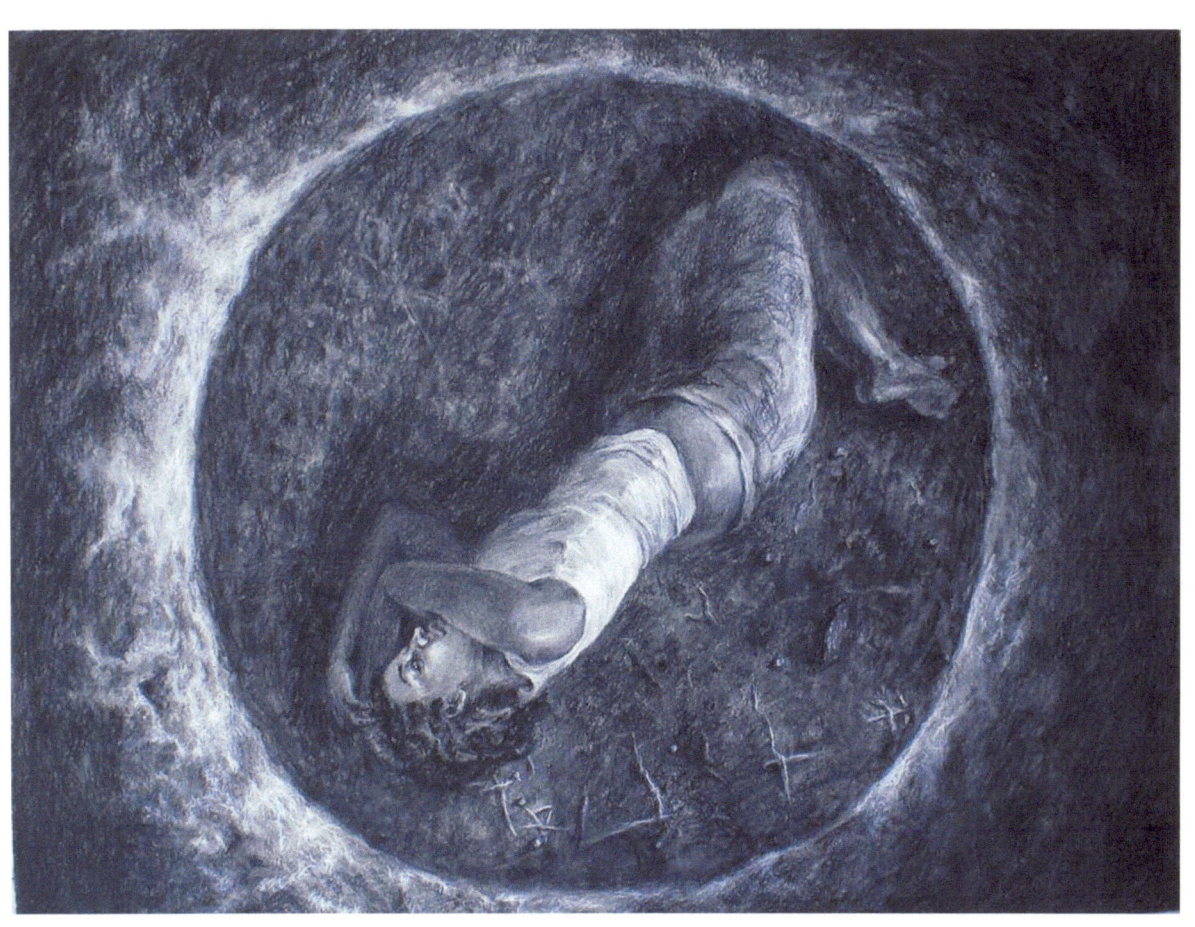

Kaleeka Bond

Primitive, charcoal on paper, 18 x 24"

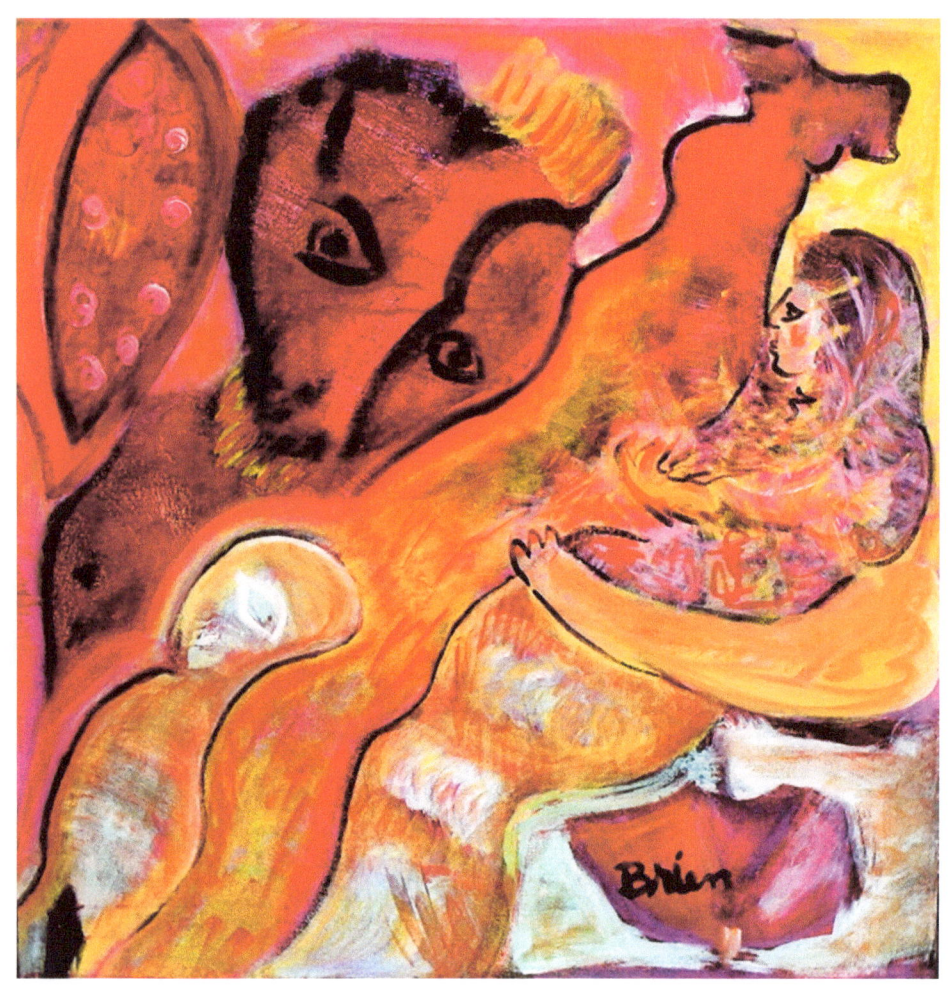

Shaktima Brien

Van Gogh, Goddess, Alien, acrylic on canvas, 24 x 24”

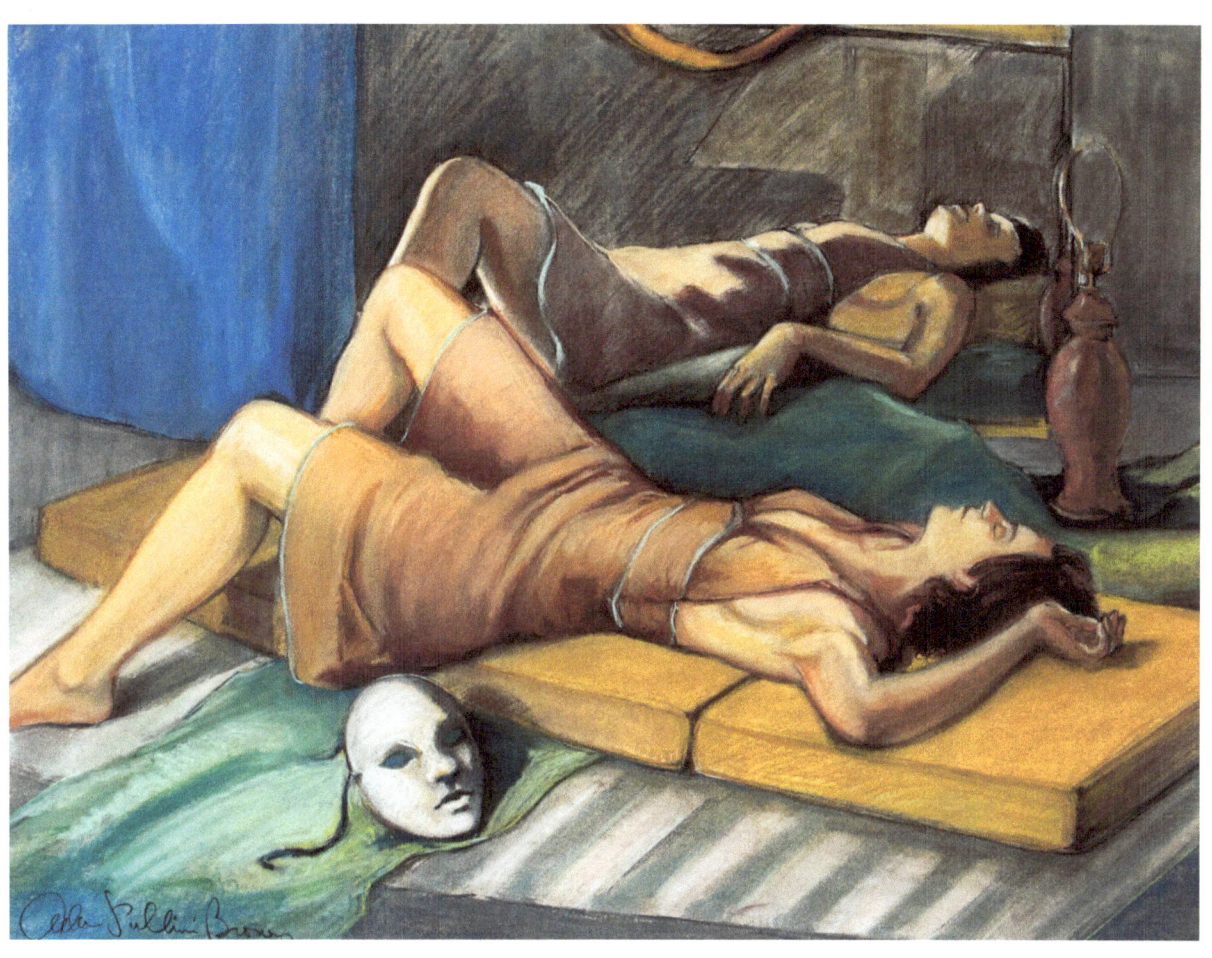

Ada Pullini Brown

Mirrored Dream, pastel on Strathmore Bristol paper, 22 x 30"

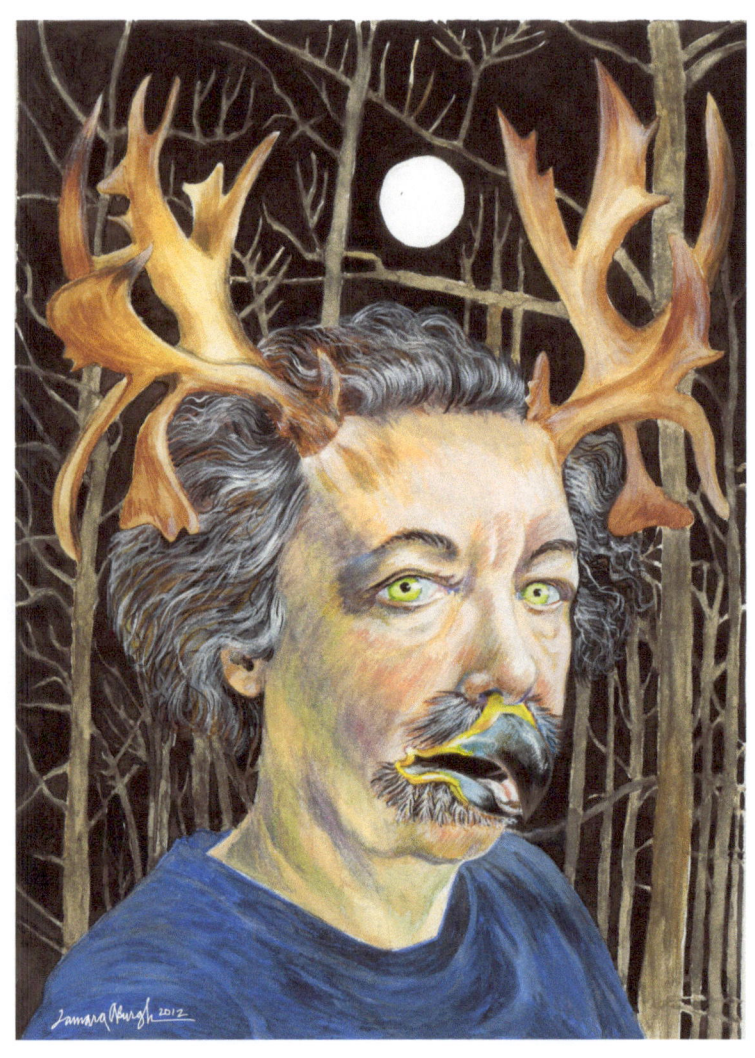

Tamara Ann Burgh

Important Things Happen in the Woods, watercolor on paper, 22 x 18"

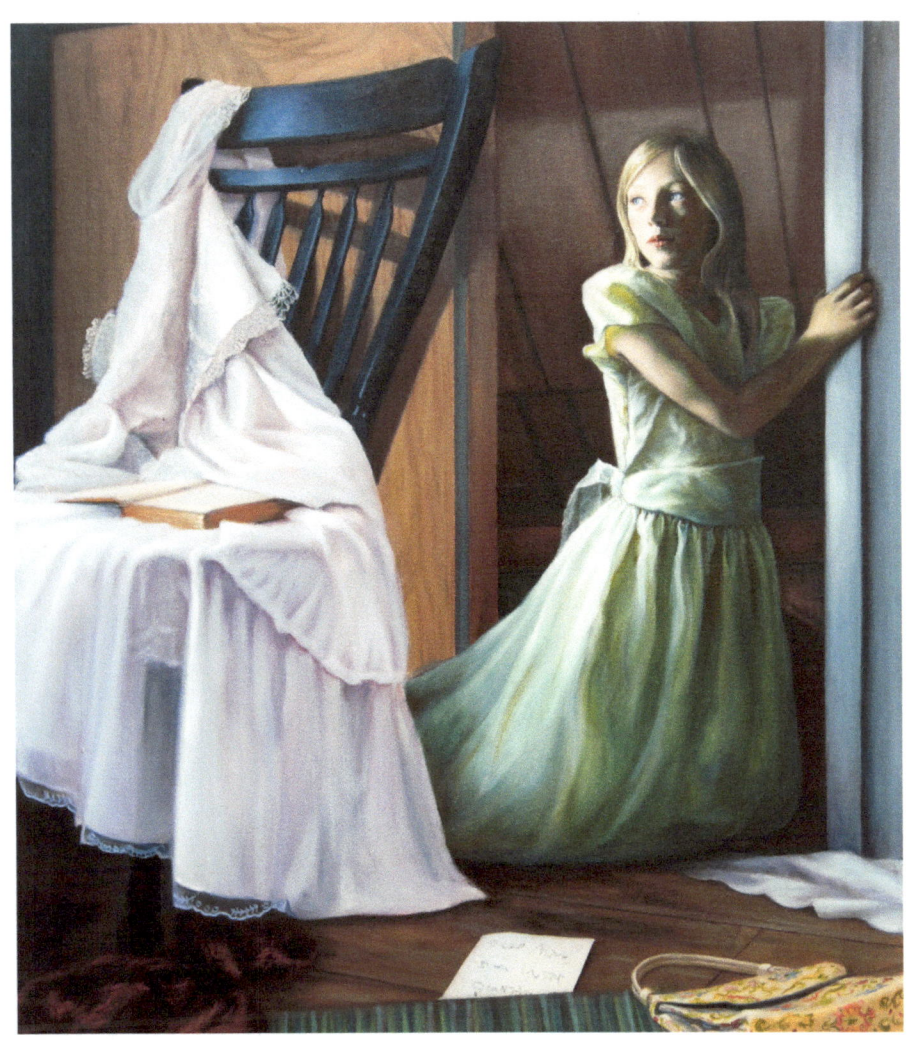

Salem Cade

Ripley's Garden, oil on canvas, 36 x 32"

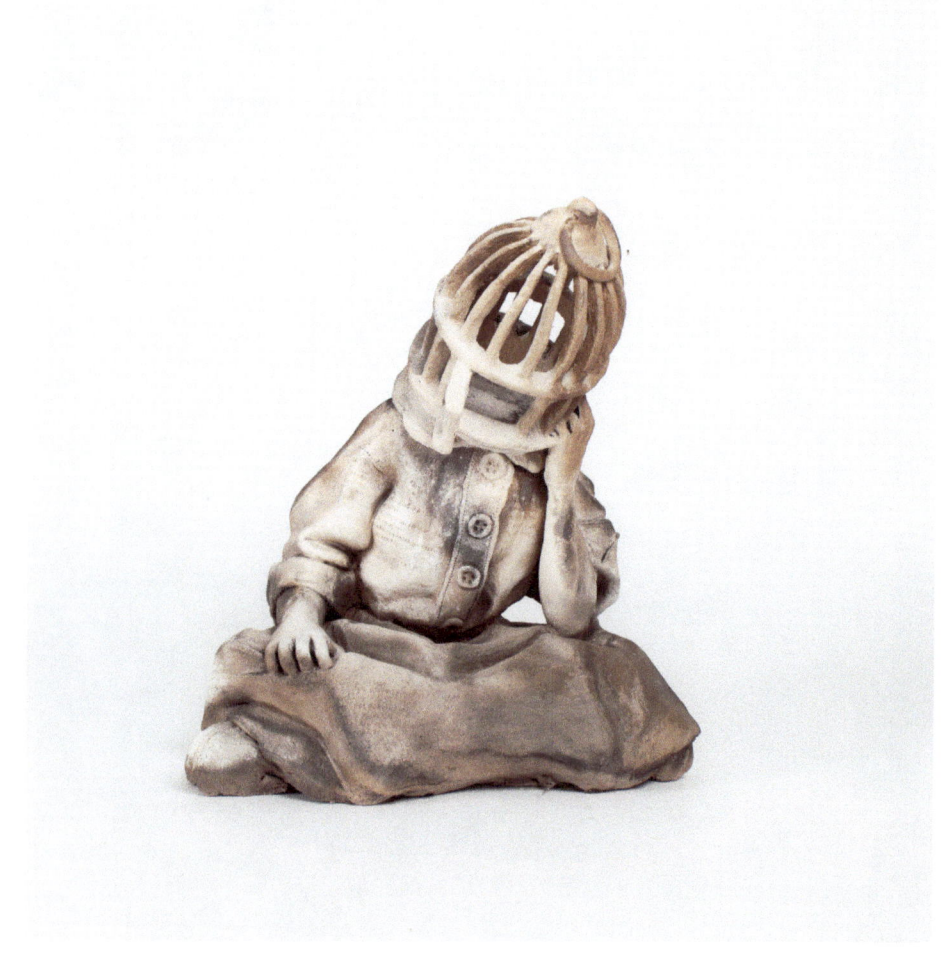

Rowena Hannan

Prokne, fired earthenware & sawdust, 12 1/2 x 11 3/8 x 9 3/4"

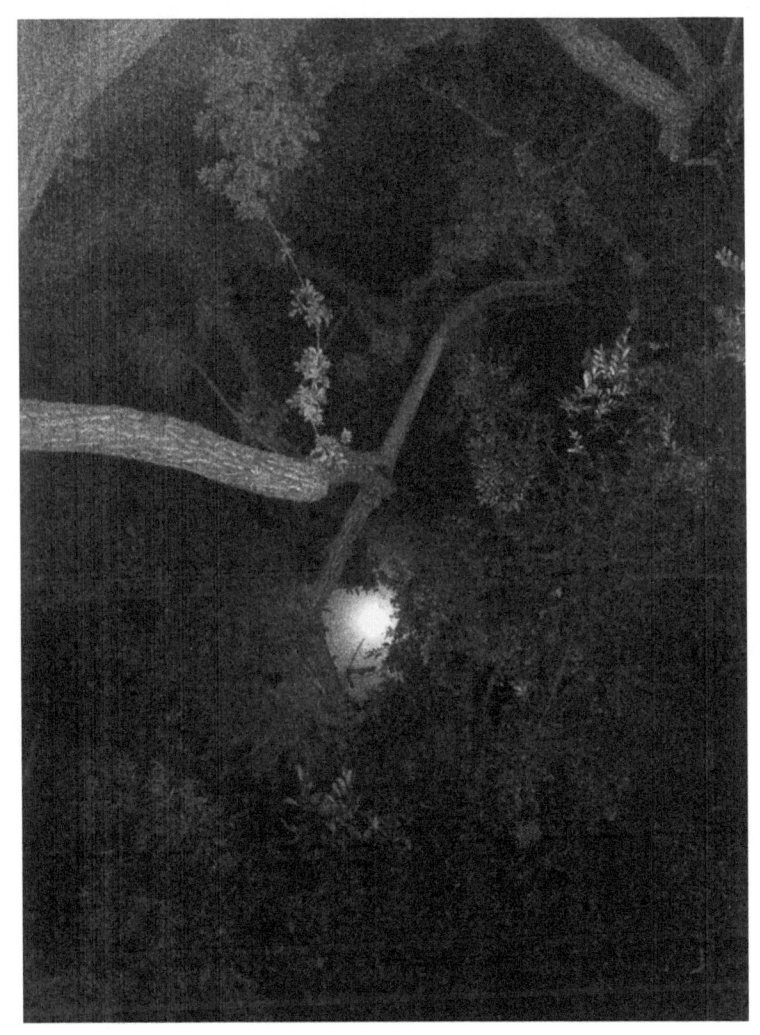

Pamela Hassell

Under The Moon, mobile digital photograph, 18 1/8 x 15 1/8"

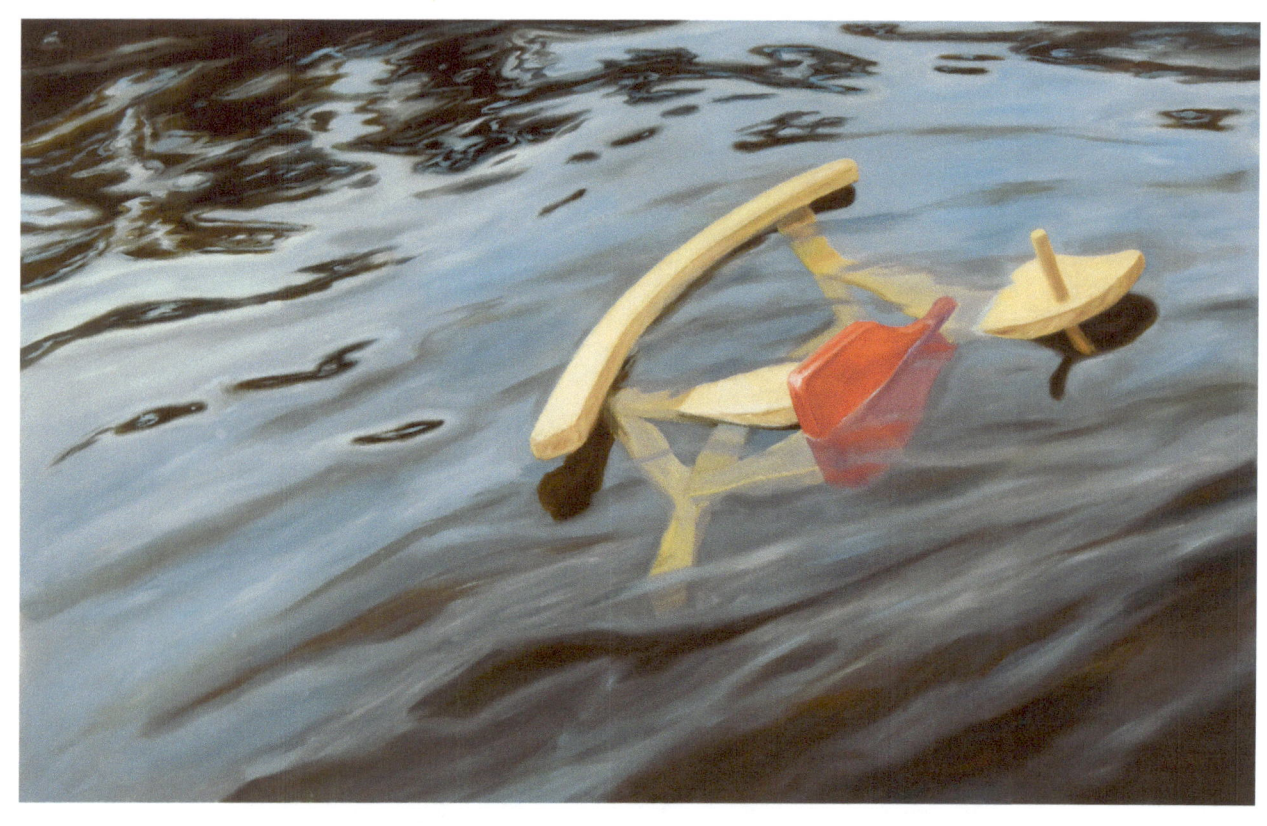

Robin Hextrum

Swept Away, oil on canvas, 34 x 56"

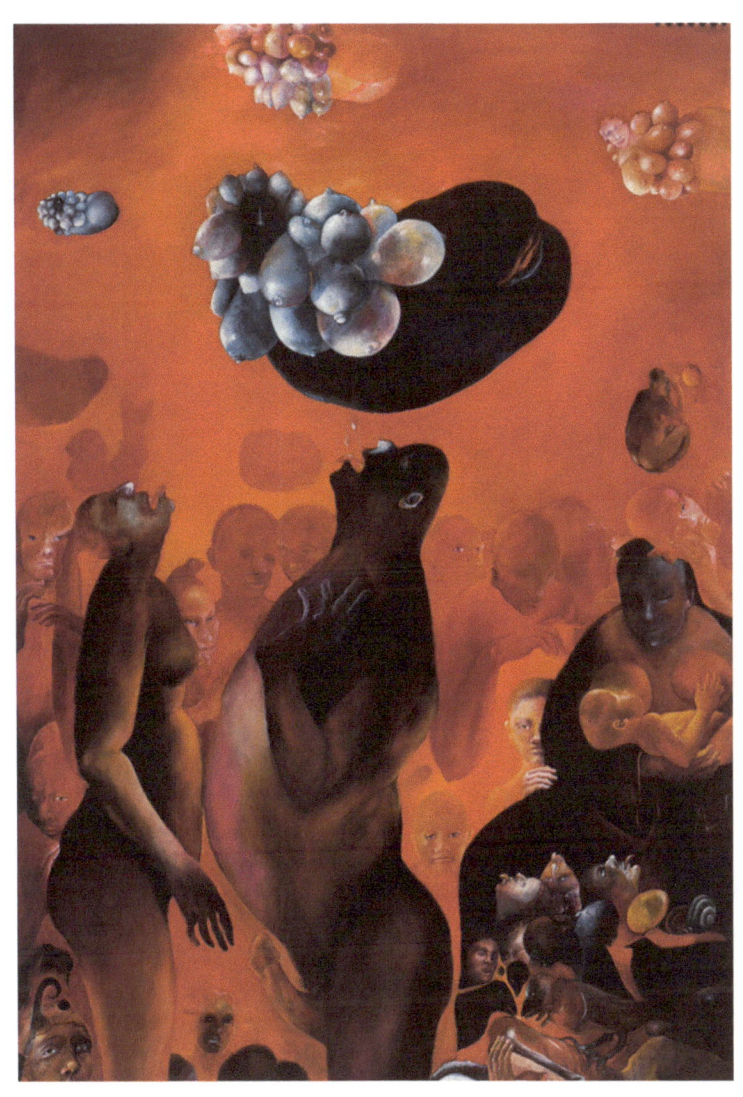

Kathryn Jacobi

Milk of Human Kindness, oil on panel, 72 x 48"

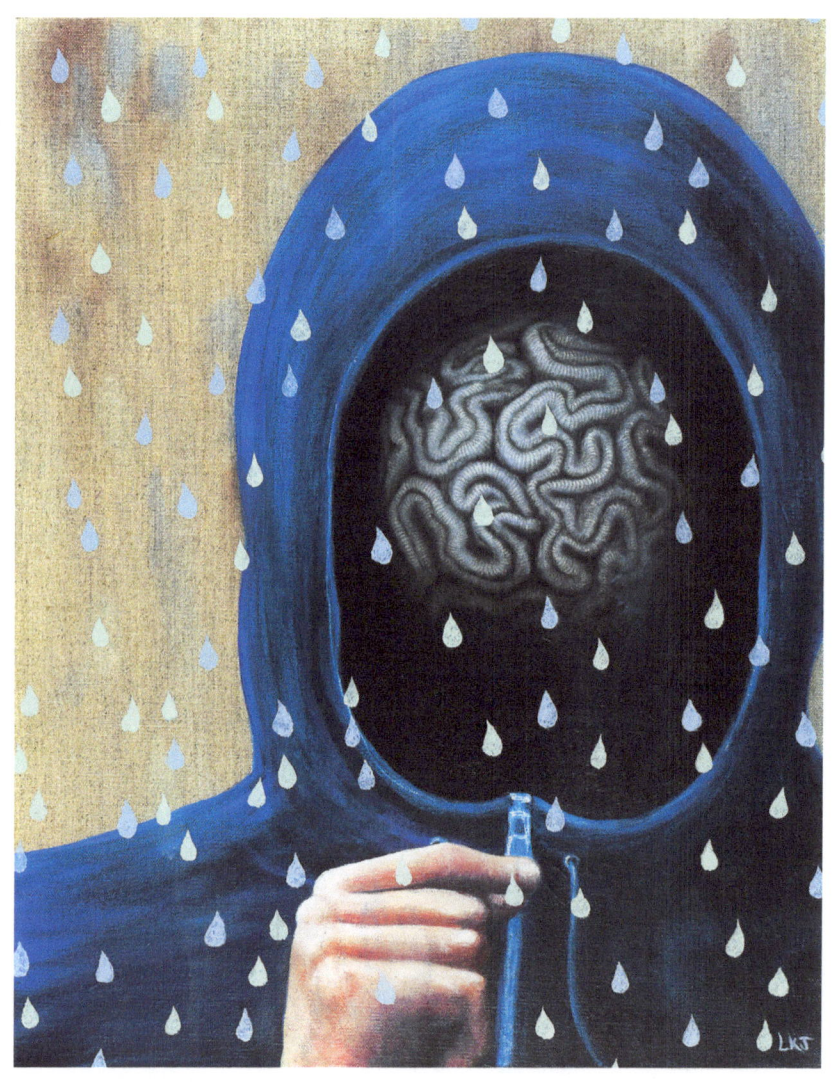

Laura K. Johnston

Never Mind the Rain, mixed media on raw linen, 20 x 16"

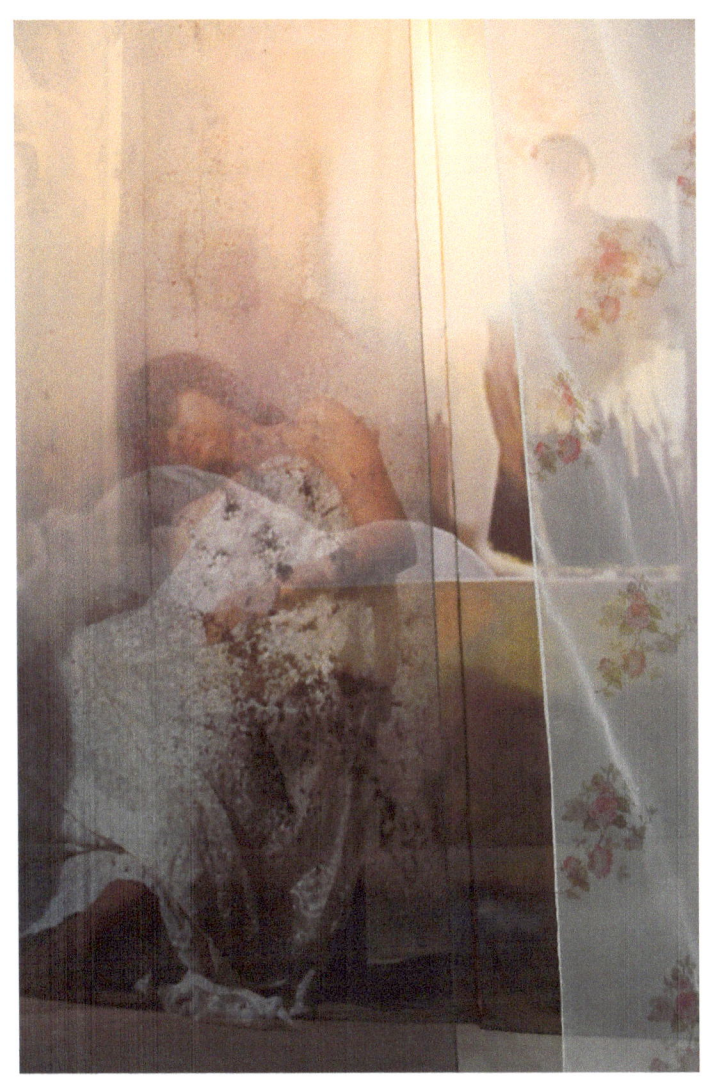

Eleni Lyra

Archangel, installation with photograph, cloth & light, 9'9" x 6'9"

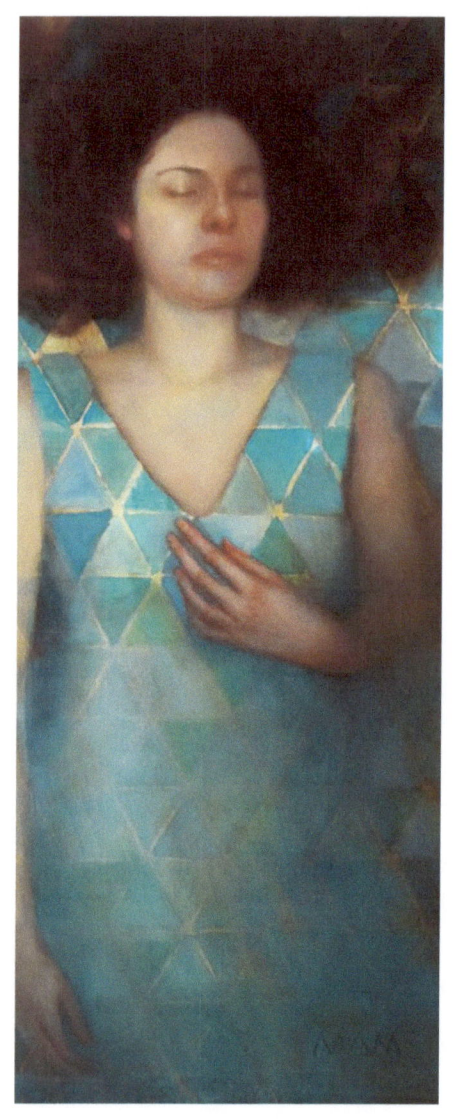

Mary Ancilla Martinez

4th Etheric, oil on panel, 22 x 9"

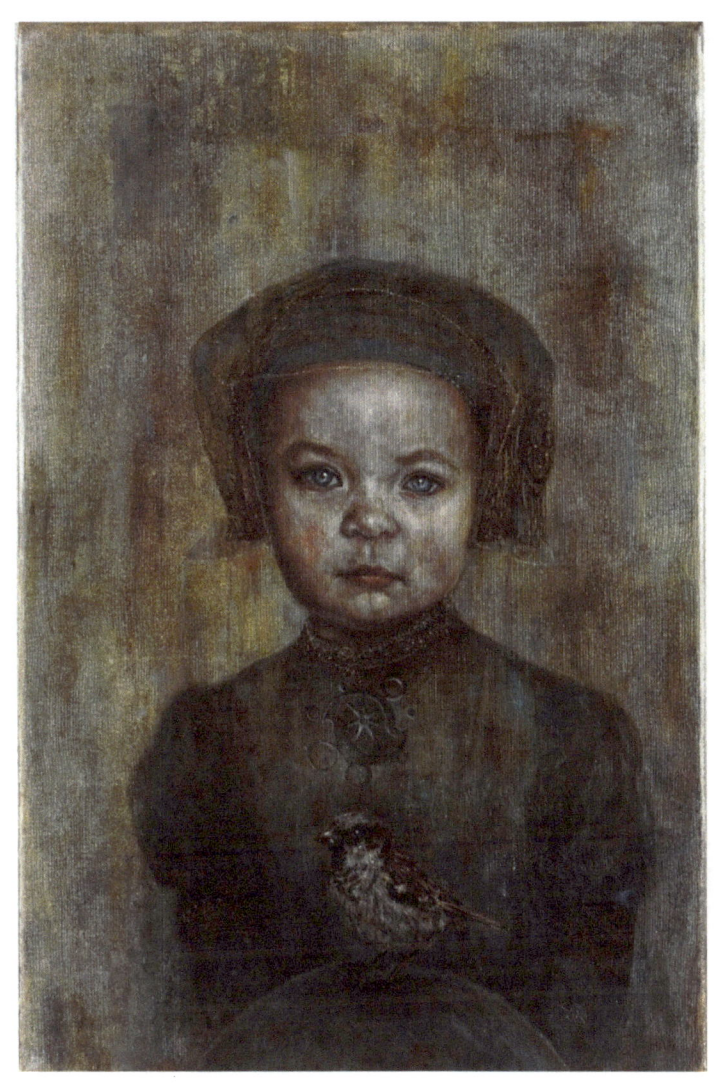

Hanneke Naterop

Dream, oil on canvas, 16 x 12"

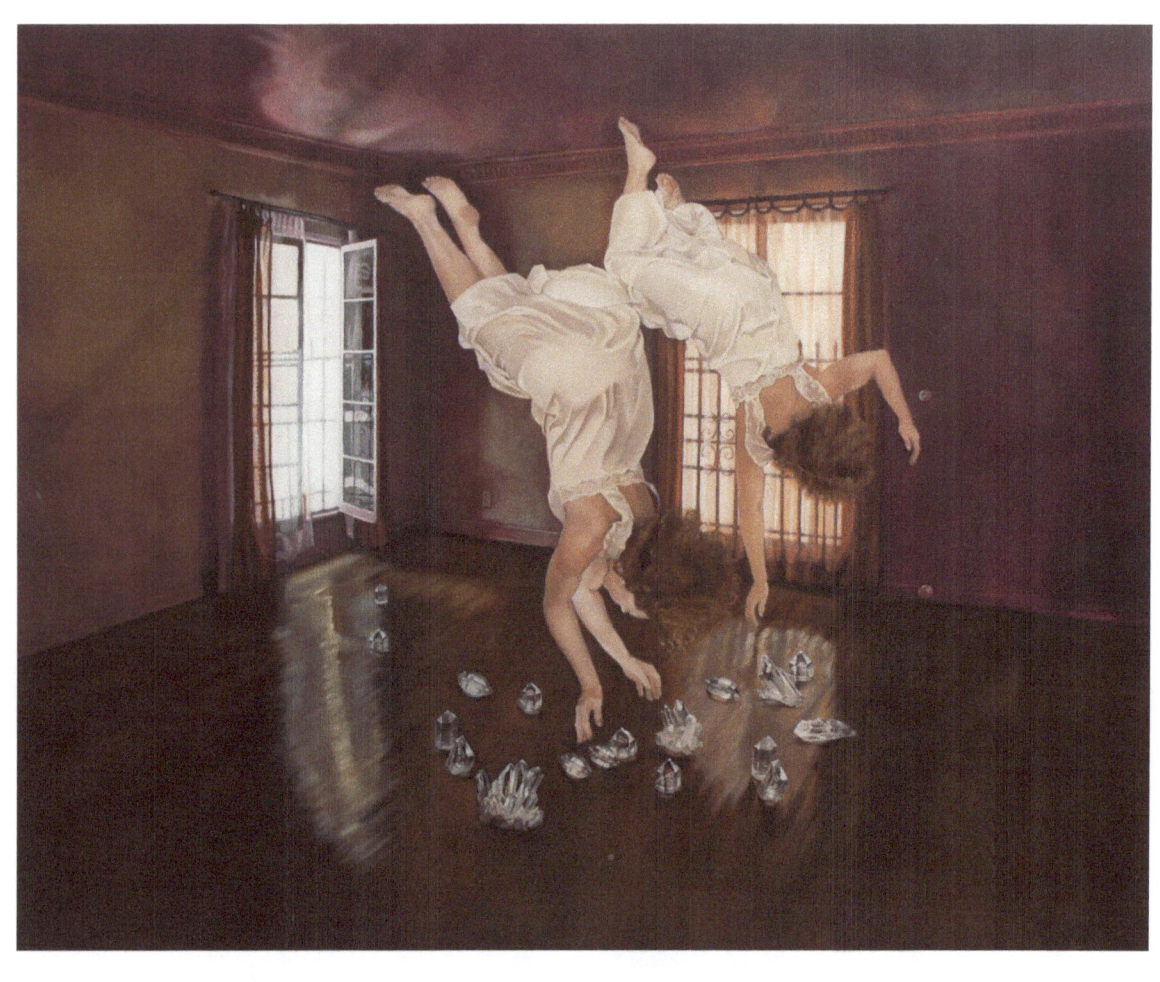

Peggy Nichols

Astral Diving for Crystals, oil on canvas, 48 x 60"

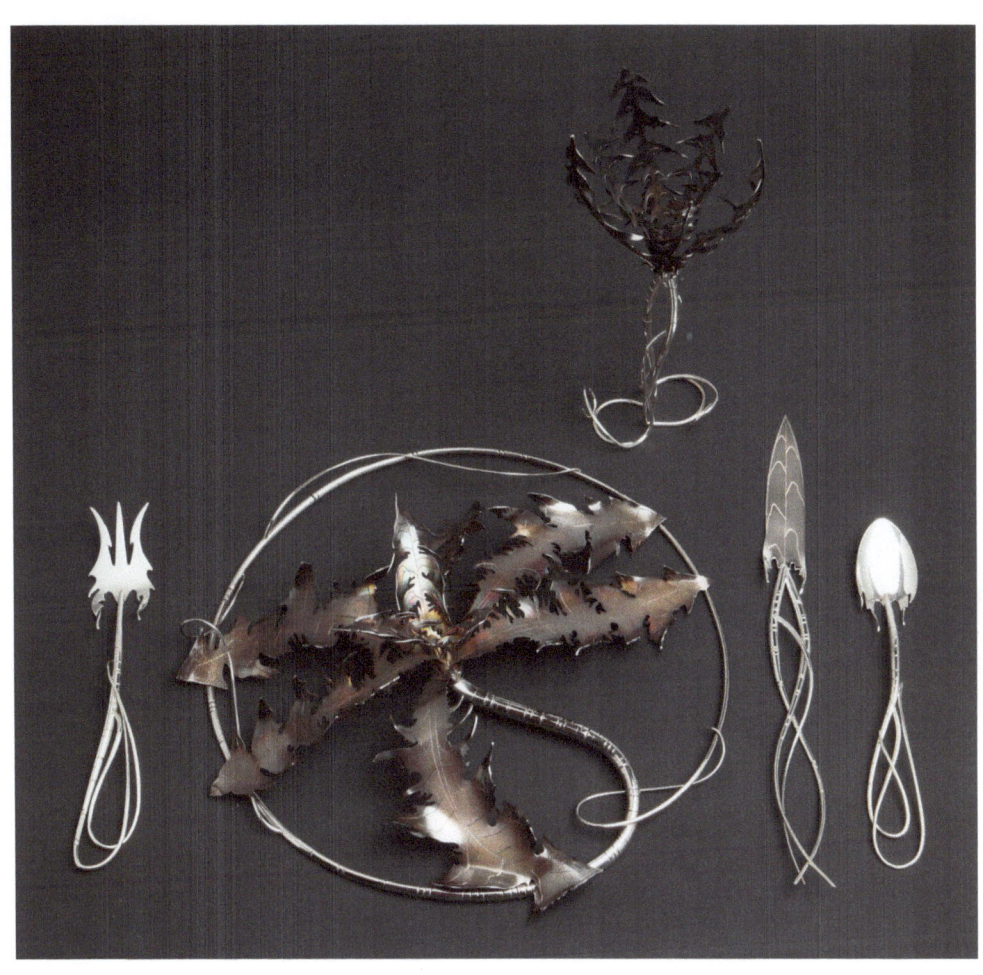

Robyn Nichols

Noxious Lawn Companion. Medicinally Complete. Beautifying the Contradiction.
sterling silver, 16 x 14 x 9"

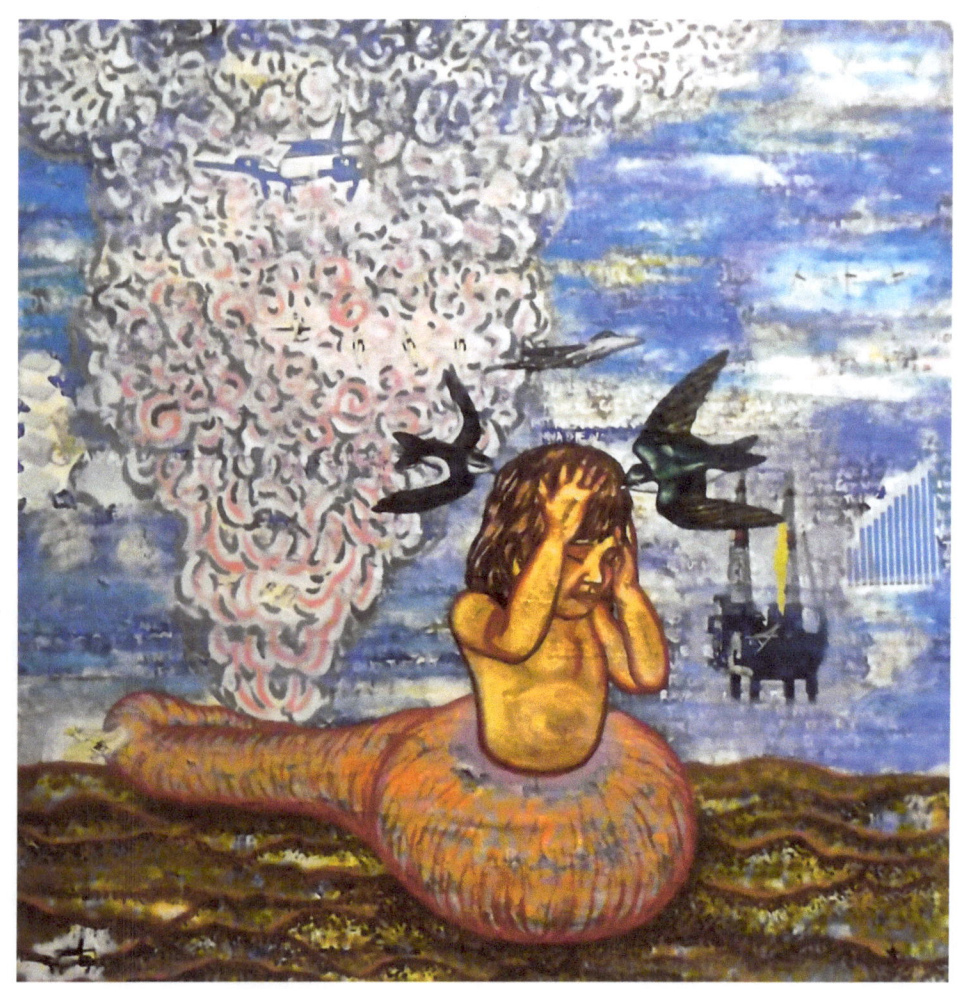

Star Padilla

War Baby, mixed media & collage on paper, 36 x 36"

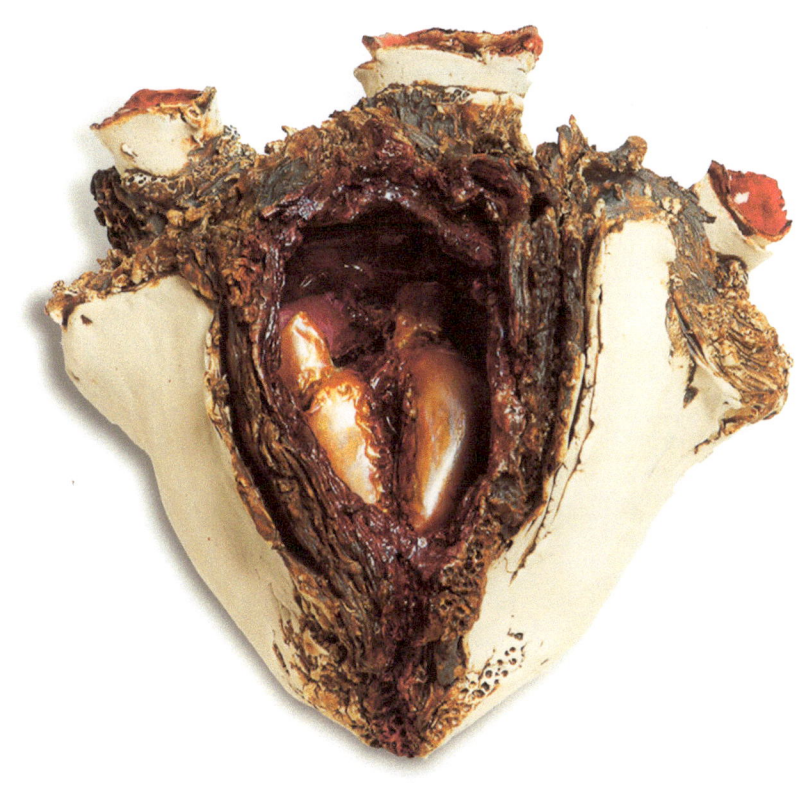

Sierra Pecheur

Resurrection Heart, porcelain, oxide, glaze & luster, 9 x 9 x 5"

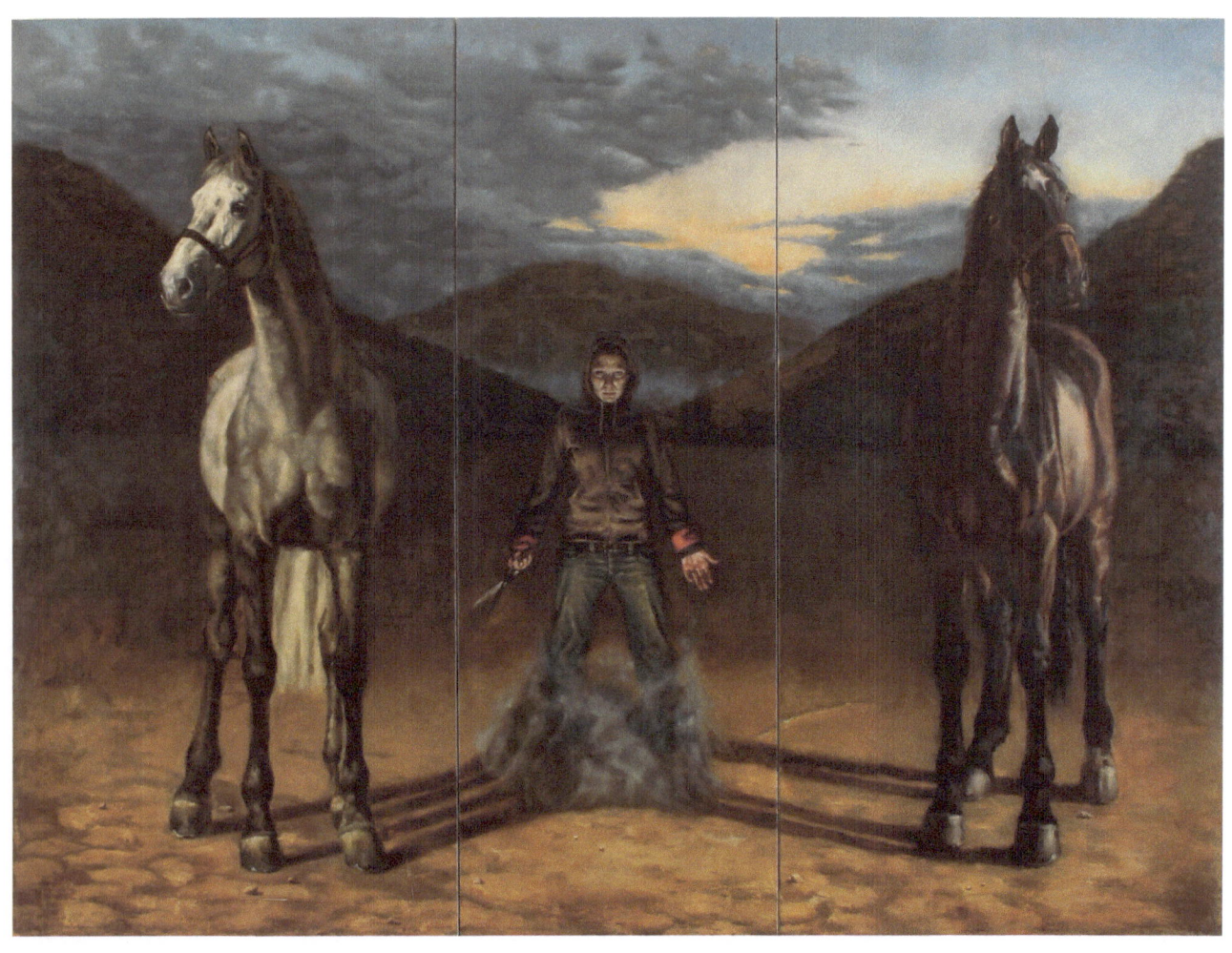

Carolin Peters

Summoned, triptych - oil on canvas, 84 x 114"

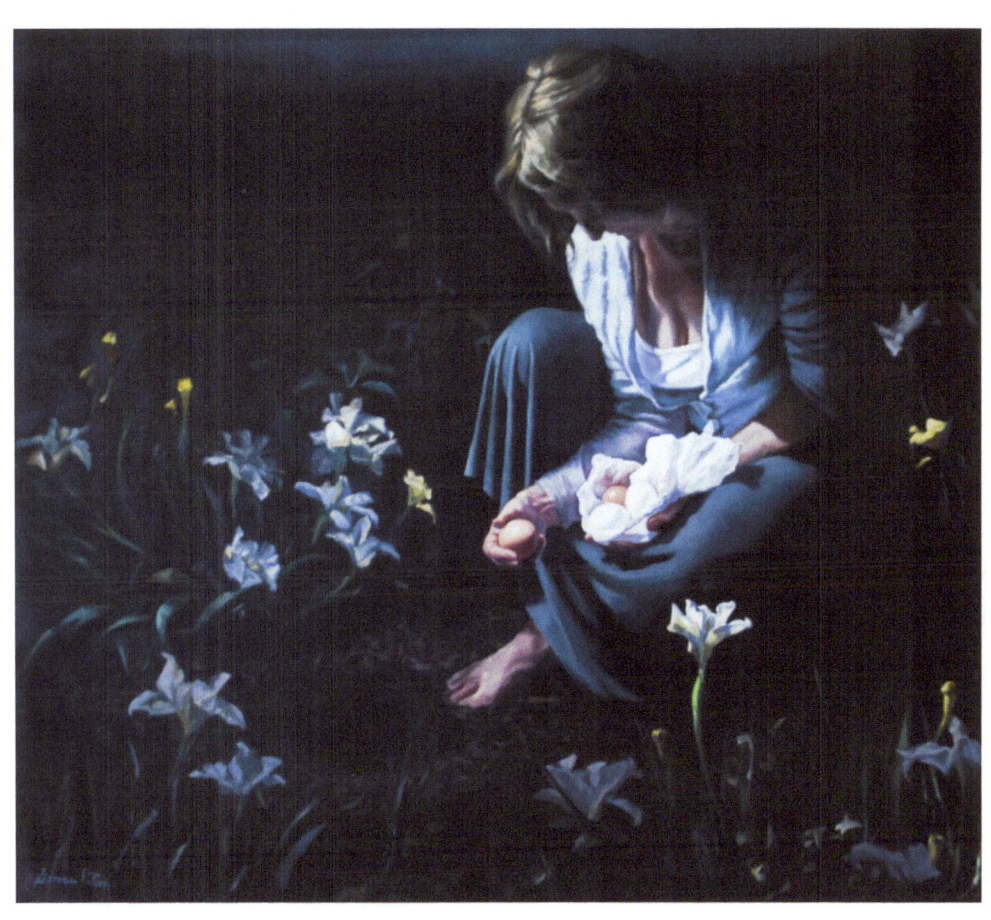

Serena Potter

All Her Cares, oil on panel, 32 x 36"

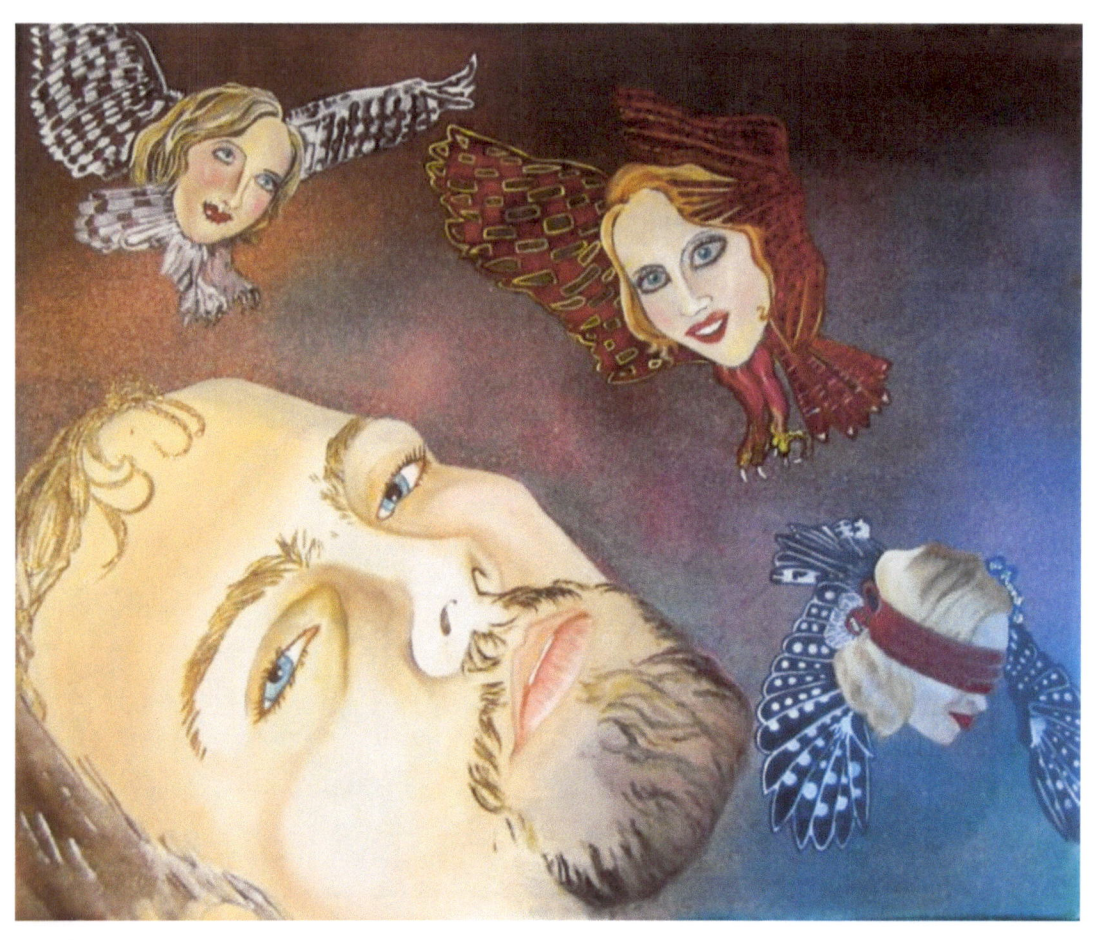

Linda Rand

Hypnopomp, oil & acrylic on canvas, 18 x 20"

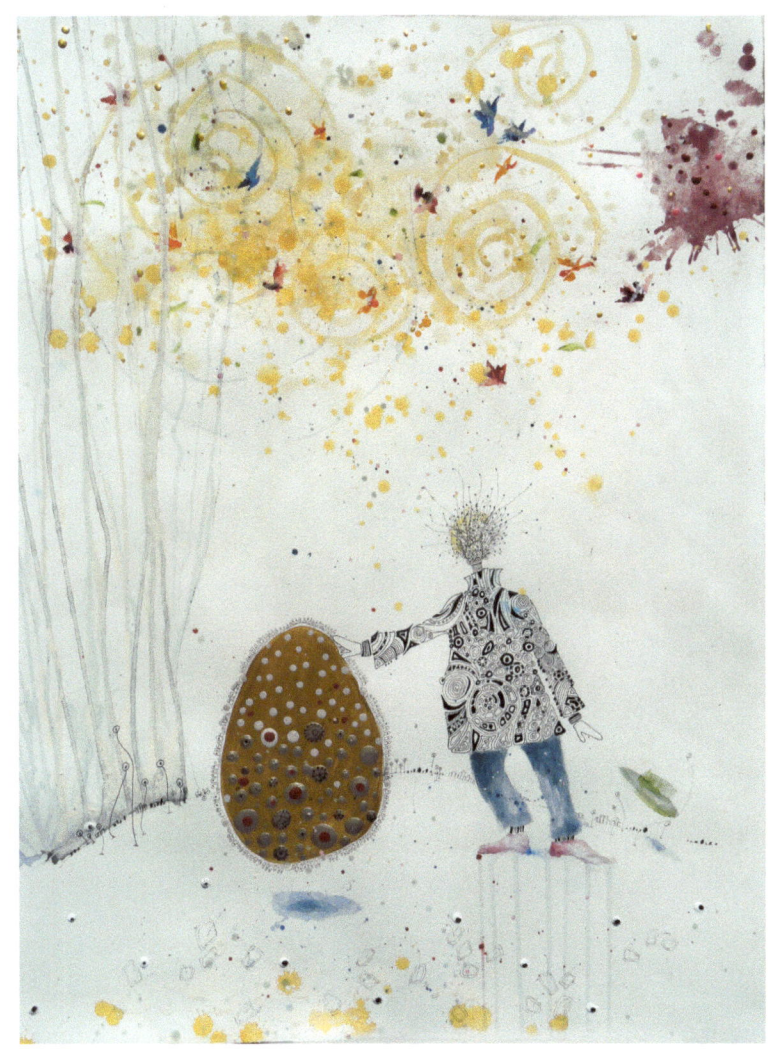

Karrie Ross

I Am The EGG! #1, acrylic, oil & ink on Arches paper, 30 x 22"

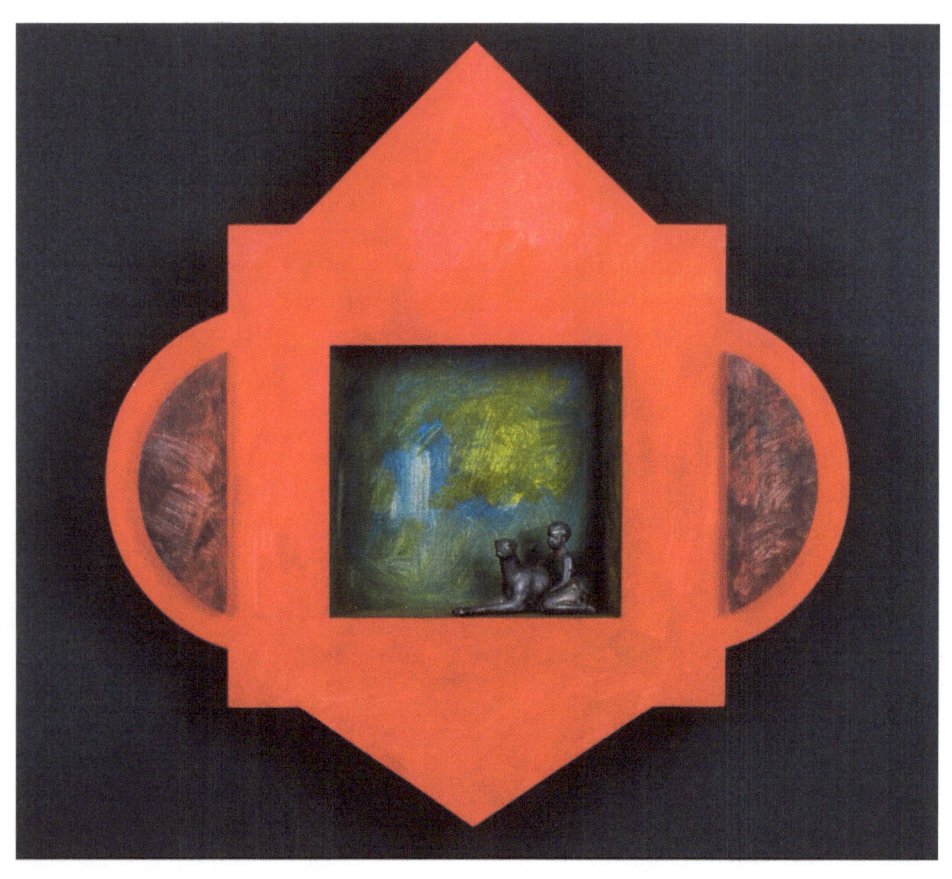

Lorraine Serena

Waiting, acrylic & wood, 26 x 25"

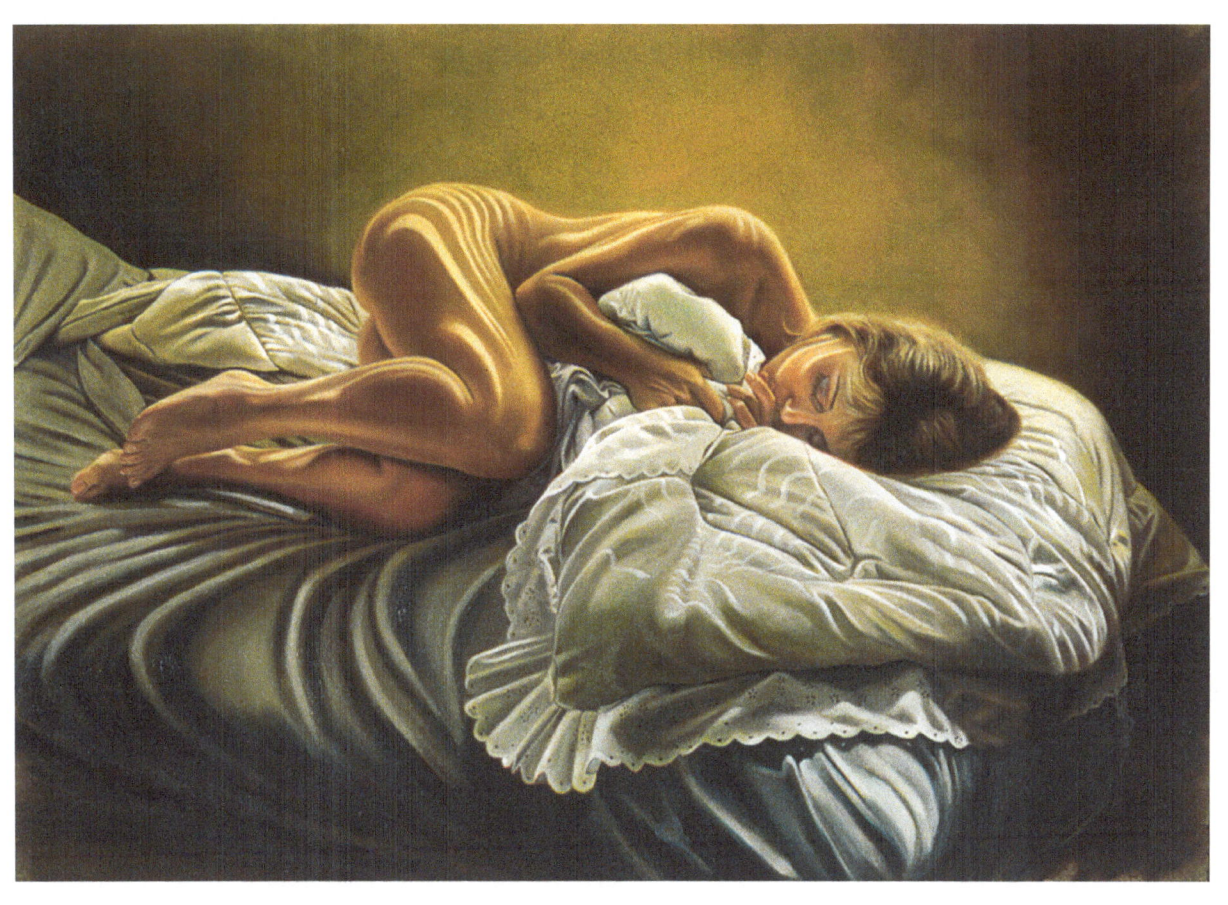

Betty Shelton

Before the Storm, oil on paper, 20 x 26"

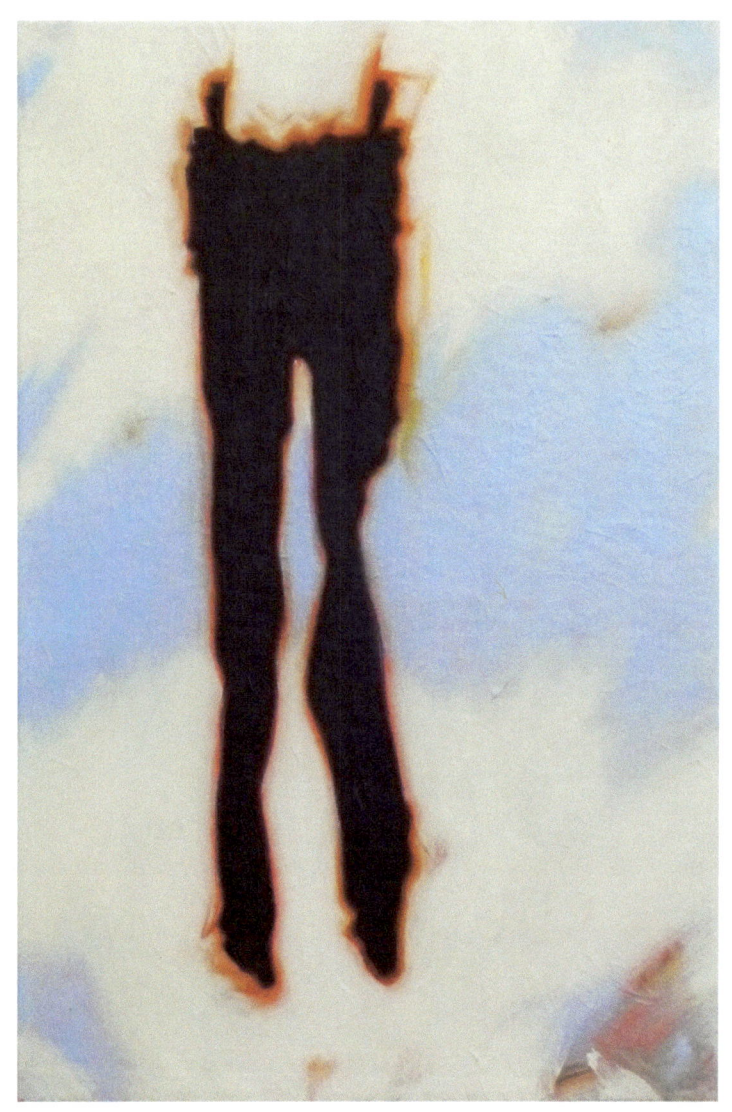

Jill Sykes

Ondoyant, oil on canvas, 18 x 12"

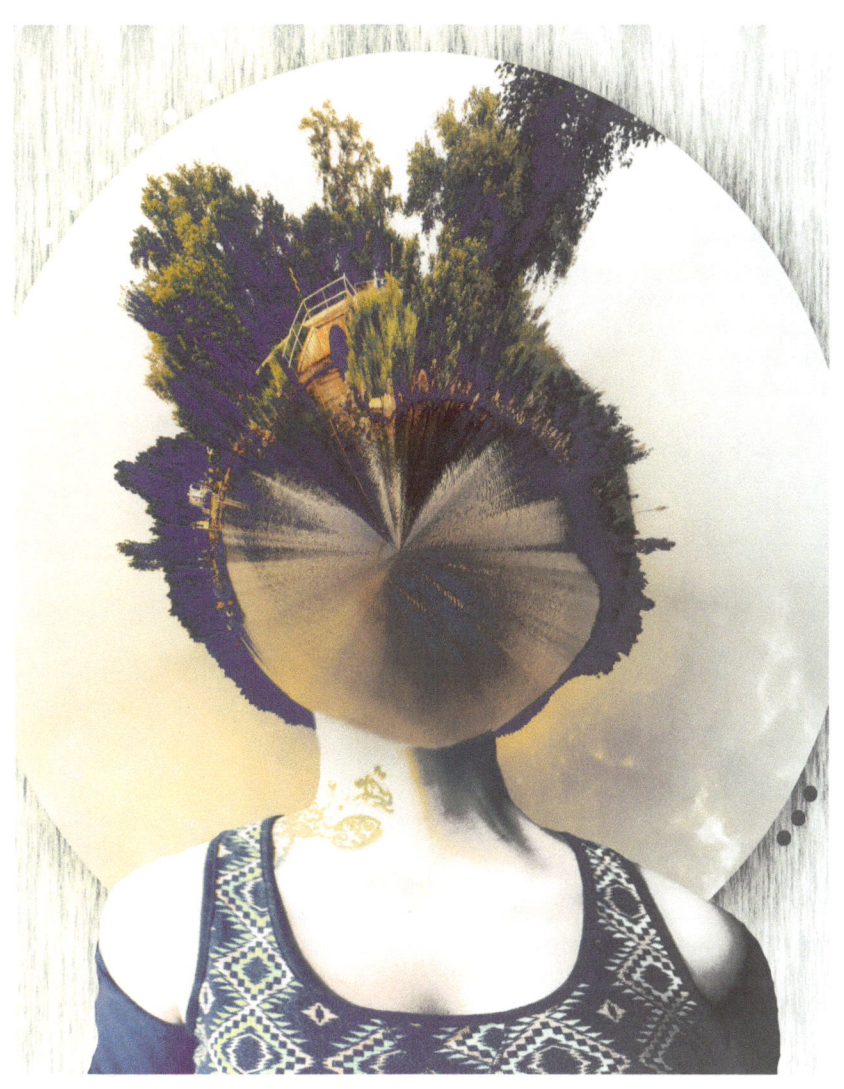

Hope Thier

Meet Me in the Yard, photography & digital collage, 10 x 8"

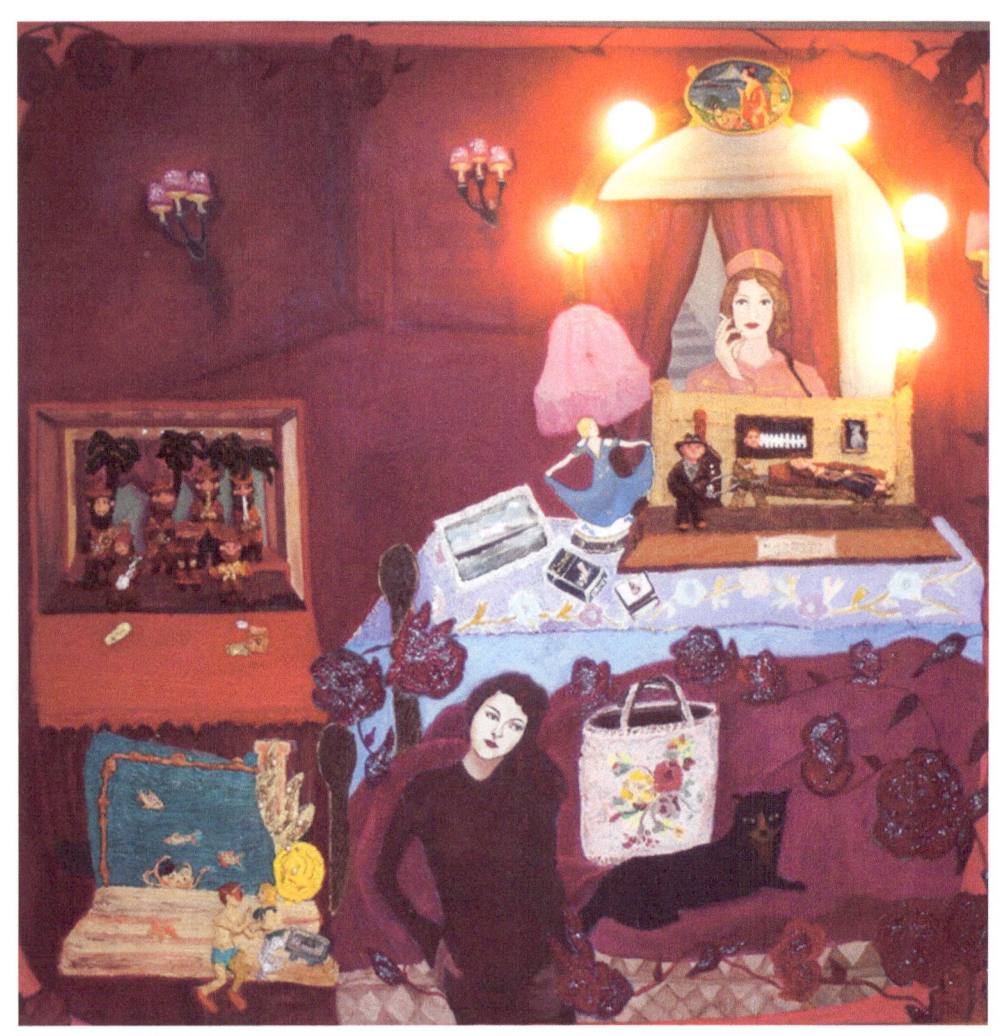

Shelli Tollman

Cigarette Girl, electric lights, collage, glitter, sewing & oil on canvas, 54 x 54"

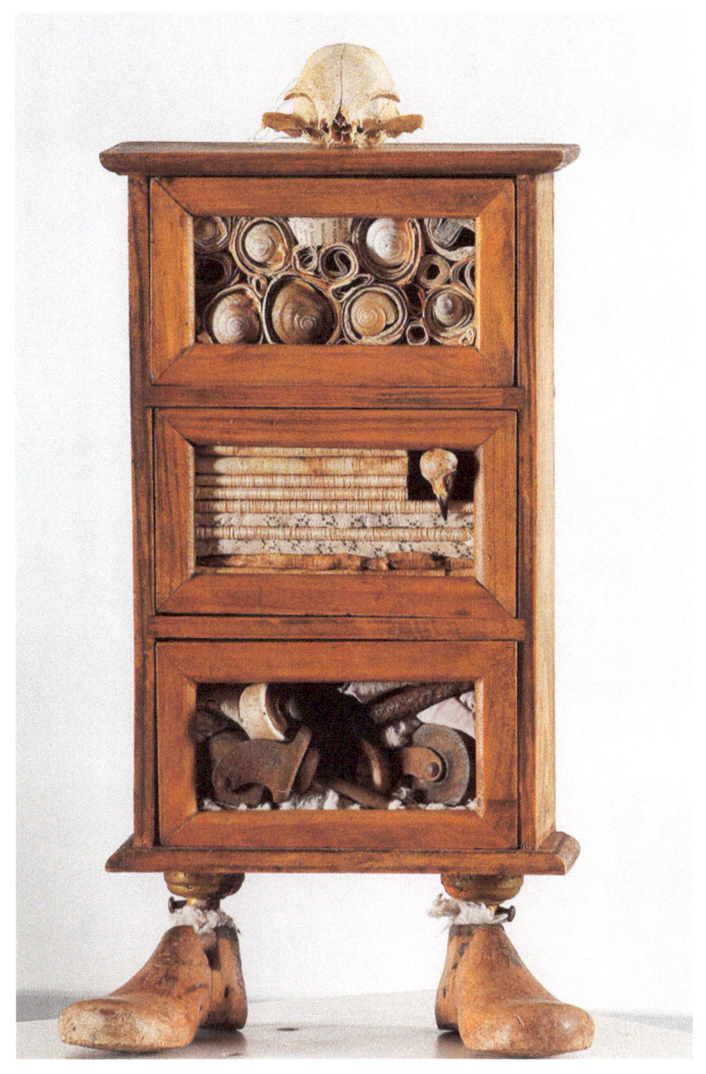

Page Turner

Tiny Toes, assemblage sculpture, 14 x 6 x 6"

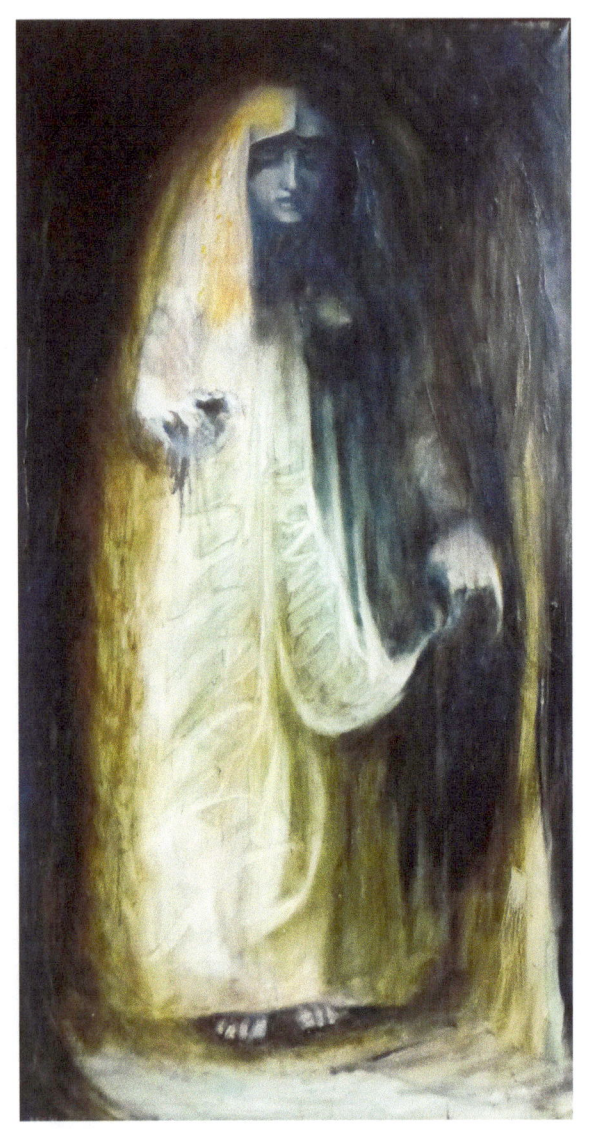

Melora Walters

The Guardian, oil on canvas, 72 x 36"

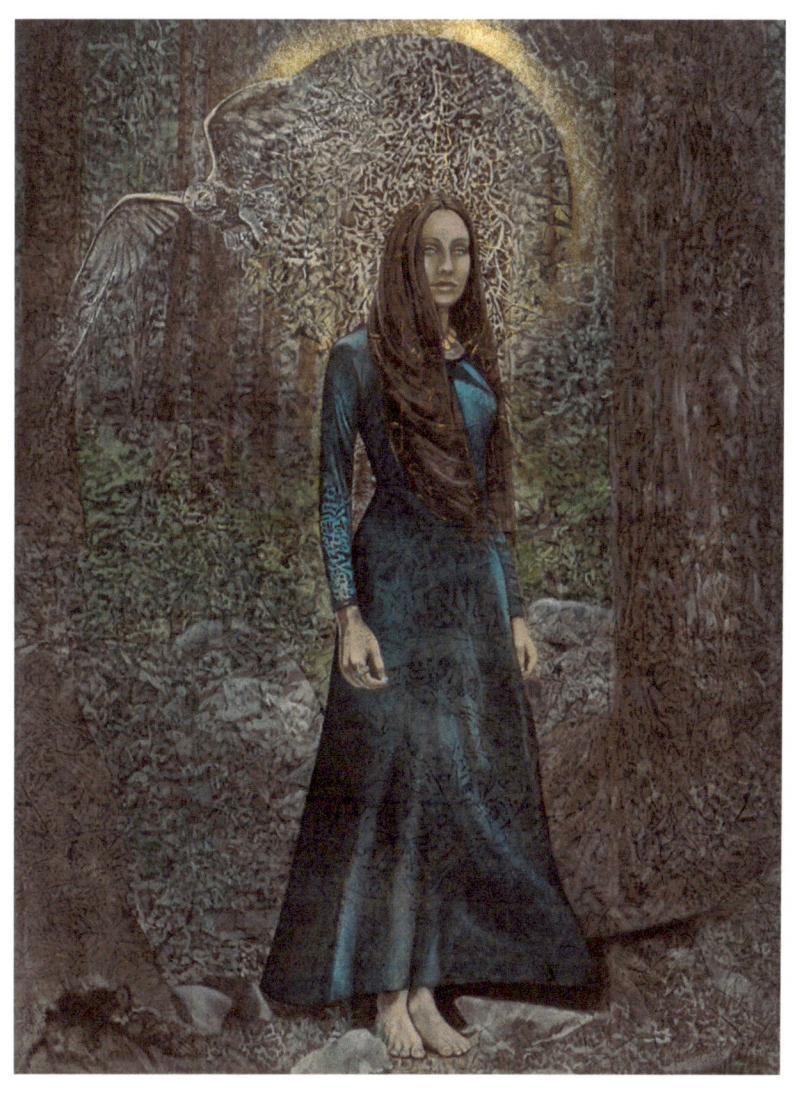

Kimberly Webber

Calming the Waters, AP#1, rice paper museum print, earth pigments & oil on panel
58 x 36"

Oneira: I Dream the Self
2nd All Women Artists Group Exhibition

Essays:
Ada Pullini Brown
Betty Ann Brown
Peggy Nichols

Front Cover Illustration: Hanneke Naterop
Back Cover Illustration: Peggy Nichols
Original Cover Design: Mary Ancilla Martinez
Catalog Design: Jill Sykes

Peggy Nichols
Studio C Gallery
Santa Fe Artist Colony
2349 So. Santa Fe Ave. Los Angeles, CA 90058